THE V

Website: www.frankpacino.com
Email: info@frankpacino.com

1st edition, May 2015

ISBN-13: 978-1512136203
ISBN-10: 1512136204

THE WISE SALESMAN

AN ENLIGHTENING MANUAL FOR A LIFE FULL OF SUCCESS AND HAPPINESS

FRANK PACINO

FRANK PACINO
— PUBLISHING —

Realize that true happiness lies within you. Waste no time and effort searching for peace and contentment and joy in the world outside. Remember that there is no happiness in having or in getting, but only in giving. Reach out. Share. Smile. Hug. Happiness is a perfume you cannot pour on others without getting a few drops on yourself.

—OG MANDINO

To the Wise Salesman hidden in you

CONTENTS

PREFACE

he Wise Salesman was born from the knowledge I gathered both in practice, through my entrepreneurial activities, and in theory, through an accurate study of the philosophy of personal success. It is from this philosophy that I extracted the principles necessary to achieve whatever one wishes in life.

This book, therefore, consists of a harmonious work containing valuable advice, secrets, and practical suggestions to help you awaken the Wise Salesman hidden within you—the concept of a salesman is to be read allegorically, as a metaphor for life. Moreover, the philosophical wisdom gradually coming to light page after page will help you understand the best attitude to have in every situation in order to effectively reach success.

The principles emerging from this book also stem from an attentive observation of the behaviours and ways of thinking of successful people: although belonging to different contexts and environments, they all share the same philosophy, which therefore seems to be universal. All successful people seem to have completely assimilated these principles, which have become a life habit clearly marking their personality.

The Wise Salesman is an "all-inclusive" self-help work: a reading for everyone who is seeking inspiration and motivation to achieve personal success in life, no matter what field is involved.

The reading of this valuable, illuminating book will offer you the great opportunity to acquire a priceless treasure of wisdom, which I hope you will be able to spend in a fruitful and virtuous way, to achieve your existential goals and reach happiness. It does not matter who you are today. Anybody can change their life and start a new one.

Frank Pacino

PROLOGUE

Every spring, a rich merchant would come to town. He was considered to be the greatest merchant in the world, and his tent was the most beautiful of all. The wind would caress it gently, spreading around perfumes, spices, flowers, and decorations. No bells would ever tinkle more sweetly at the touch of the spring breeze than those hanging from the sunshade of his tent, and the people rushed towards it, enchanted by wonder. The merchant, they said, knew the whole world, and every year he carried with him something marvelous as a token of the places he had visited and the adventures he had faced—in deserts, valleys, arduous peaks, and steep slopes. His tent was a mirror of all the delights in the world. This was his way of bringing to the others a bit of India, a bit of China, a bit of America—a bit of world. Around his tent, there would always be frenetic activity: people walking in and out, and everywhere, small groups eagerly waiting to enter. Sometimes, they had to wait for hours before being received in the tent.

The business of the merchant flourished, and in addition to the great material riches he managed to gain, he loved being always able to fulfil people's wishes. As a matter of fact, it never occurred to anybody to ask the merchant for something he could not eventually give them. At times, the merchant had exactly what the people desired. At other times, on the contrary, his brilliant and persuasive speech could convince the customers that what he had available was exactly what they had been looking for. Often, the objects he had for sale came with an enchanting story. He was well aware that people did not simply want to buy objects; many also wished for a story that would make them happy. So he happened to offer them a silk tapestry that once belonged to a Chinese emperor, or a work of art skilfully painted by a great master, or a book whose paper was many centuries old. And the people would go home happy, carrying something that had the power to make them dream.

One day, among the many people huddling around his tent, a boy came up. His father had sent him there to learn the secrets of the greatest merchant of all time, and he had come a very long way to reach that marvelous place. He waited for hours before it was his turn to be received. The meeting, for the young boy, turned out to be something magical. From that moment on, he started on a new path of growth. What he had been until that day did not matter anymore because a new life awaited him, a new destiny had to be fulfilled: he would excel in every situation of his life, pursuing the accomplishment of a goal, his own goal. And this is how the Wise Salesman was born.

Chapter 1

MOTIVATION: THE POWER OF ACTING NOW AND THE MIRACLE OF ENTHUSIASM

The Wise Salesman knows the importance of motivation, as the expression of an extraordinary force able to multiply immensely his probability of success and therefore his own value. Motivation, as a matter of fact, can make the difference between success and failure in the life of anybody. Even before preparation, ability, and experience, motivation represents an invisible power, often wild and unrestrained, that is indispensable in order to move forward.

When the strength of motivation pushes him forward on his path, the Wise Salesman is not afraid to fail. The height of the goals he strives for does not scare him in the least. He convinces himself that he is strong and that he will succeed, in a sublime and winning moment of self-motivation. Nothing can stop him. Nothing can trouble him in the arena of competition, since he believes in himself so strongly. He is sure that, conditions and opportunities being equal, he would obtain way more satisfying results than those salesmen who are crushed under the weight of demotivation and are inevitably condemned to failure.

Motivation consists of many internal factors in the soul of the Wise Salesman. It is a system of forces and phenomena that, all together, decisively influence his actions and his behaviour, allowing him, with a positive mental attitude, to achieve the success he had hoped for from the start.

There are two factors leading to a positive mental attitude in the Wise Salesman: the power of acting now and enthusiasm.

Acting now is the impulse the Wise Salesman has to act immediately, without ever waiting for tomorrow. It is a need that originates from the depths of his soul, where a virtuous flame burns pushing him towards action. Acting now, for the Wise Salesman, is more than an inner need. It is a duty. He is well aware that he cannot postpone action and that procrastination is one of the evils of humanity, leading people to sink into abysses of failure and mediocrity. Fear and hesitation are alien to him. His heart is brave. Idleness is his enemy because it kills time. After all, he knows very well that all the achievements of mankind, our so-called "progress," derive from productivity. The Wise Salesman cannot wait for tomorrow, because tomorrow is indefinite and elusive, as indefinite as his dreams, expectations, and ambitions. These are like stars in the dark of the night: they can guide and inspire him, but they still do not physically belong to him. Acting in the present is the only, and therefore most valuable, instrument for the Wise Salesman to reach the peaks of success and finally touch the stars. They may shine so far away that they seem impossible to grasp, but one day he will conquer them. Acting now is the only concrete instrument he has, because he has learned to face challenges as they show up. He never believed those patient men who kept telling him, "You must learn to wait." Sure, if he could live forever, time would teach him everything, but he cannot afford the luxury of eternity. The Wise Salesman does not procrastinate because he knows of only one right moment to do things, and that moment is now. If he hesitated, waiting for the perfect moment, he would never achieve success. He has the power to choose his own destiny, and therefore, he never waits for things to happen but rather acts to make them happen—albeit with a pinch of folly, because in war, just like in love, it is impossible to foresee everything.

The Wise Salesman is not naive and never makes the mistake to believe that success should be at his fingertips. He knows that sales, just like any other activity in life, cannot escape the inexorable law of nature, which says that every goal requires a specific time. An olive tree takes a hundred years to prosper. But the Wise Salesman knows that, however long the way may be, every success is the sum of many small actions, constantly carried out day by day and deriving from positive habits. Without today's actions, no success, small as it may be, can be accomplished tomorrow. This is why today is an essential tool to use, and since the hourglass of time never gives back the days gone by, as much profit as possible should be made today. The Wise Salesman knows the trick to be able to act immediately: he tries to live each day as if it were the last one. Wasting time would throw his life away. And he does not want to lose even one drop of his life, nor waste time and energy complaining about yesterday's failures. He cannot travel back in time; he cannot be young again or live past situations once more to fix his mistakes. No, he cannot do any of this. Yesterday is gone once and for all. But the future is out of reach too. Why should he overlook today, that which is, for the sake of tomorrow, that which might be? Can the problems of tomorrow bother him today? Can the happiness of tomorrow light up his heart today? Can the success of tomorrow show up today? No, none of this is possible. So he forgets about yesterday and does not think about tomorrow. And he enjoys the most what he has: the present, his only eternity, an invaluable good. Today he accomplishes all his personal and professional duties, offering himself as sacrifice to life and the quest to excel. Tomorrow, all of this might be useless. If today were really his last day, it would be the best day of his life, the greatest of his triumphs! And should it not be his last day, he would welcome the new dawn with immense joy, grateful for the priceless gift of a new day. At times, though, he believes he does not deserve so much happiness: He knows the unhappiness of the other people. He knows the solitude, the frustration, and the failure that always accompany most of mankind, and he comes to think that the hours given to him today might be an undeserved gift. In those moments, he asks himself: "Why was I given the opportunity to live one more day while others much better than me are gone?" So he reflects, and comes to realize that his life must have a goal to accomplish and that the time in his hands is but a precious opportunity to become the person he wishes to be. A new life awaits him, and one day he will pay back everything, offering his successes to those he always loved. This is the way he overcomes the feeling of guilt, and he stops asking himself pointless questions.

The colleagues of the Wise Salesman comment, "How lucky he is!" And truly, the Wise Salesman obtains much more than what his performance would deserve. But his only luck is being motivated. His success is never achieved by fortune or by chance. It is rather the outcome of his way of thinking and acting. A salesman may be the most cultured person, may have studied at the most prestigious universities and attended the best seminars about sales, but if he has a negative attitude about things, he most certainly will fail. The Wise Salesman, on the contrary, always has a positive mental attitude, which influences his thoughts as well as his expression and body language, perfecting his ability to persuade. The Wise Salesman is never a prey in the arena of competition; he is always a predator, hungry and combative. A lion, when hungry, acts immediately, hunting for food. If it did not act, it would perish. This is why it does not hesitate, nor does it wait to reflect. It is often the strongest and the quickest who win fights. This is what the Wise Salesman does: he bravely faces his customers, knocks on closed doors, and does not fear rejection, unlike the unsuccessful salesman, who tends to give up or procrastinate, a prey of fear and hesitation. The Wise Salesman tries out all paths, even the hardest and steepest ones. It is this courage that leads him to victory. Unlike the unsuccessful salesman, he never thinks, "This visit is useless." He knows the laws of statistics and knows how to use them to his benefit, avoiding setting limitations on himself. As a matter of fact, he believes that opportunities for success hide everywhere and in every moment, and therefore, he is not afraid to explore paths no one ever dared to take. He never allows imaginary obstacles to overwhelm him. His imagination focuses only on positive and optimistic thoughts, sustained by a mentality that sees obstacles as something meant to be overcome. He welcomes difficulties too, because they are a challenge. The reward, a just and valuable reward, will be greater confidence in himself. The Wise Salesman masters his thoughts. As the captain of his own soul, he is the master of his own destiny as well.

When the Wise Salesman starts a new working day, one great light shines upon him, the light of enthusiasm. This is the invisible flame that lights up his spirit, pushing him towards action and promoting his positive mental attitude. This is what gives him hope, courage, and self-confidence. He is well aware that nothing great was ever accomplished without enthusiasm. Enthusiasm stimulates initiative, both in thought and action, overcoming laziness and fatigue. An apparently lazy man is nothing but a man without enough motivation to light up his enthusiasm. The Wise Salesman uses the overwhelming power of enthusiasm to fight fear, doubt, and uncertainty, creating a positive and favourable environment instead. Enthusiasm allows him to talk with more decisiveness and fascinate his listeners, easily captivating them with his words. When he talks, he transmits passion and excites the spirit of his listeners, deeply touching their hearts. How contagious enthusiasm is! At times, it even makes the Wise Salesman appear more prepared than he actually is, so that he exerts still greater influence on his customers. Enlivened by his passion and his positive attitude, they listen attentively without ever interrupting him. Even a weak or trivial argument could become interesting and engaging if presented with enthusiasm, whereas cold eloquence cannot sell anything. The colleagues of the Wise Salesman wonder: "How can he possibly be always this enthusiastic?" The Wise Salesman knows the secret to renew enthusiasm. It is a simple but magical technique, within everybody's reach. To be enthusiastic, one must act with enthusiasm. The Wise Salesman always tries to be enthusiastic and is rewarded for his efforts by genuinely becoming enthusiastic. This is his miracle, and it happens every day.

Don't wait; the time will never be just right. Start where you stand, and work with whatever tools you may have at your command, and better tools will be found as you go along.

—NAPOLEON HILL

Chapter 2

OBSESSIVE DESIRE AND DEFINITENESS OF PURPOSE

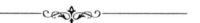

The desires of the Wise Salesman are different from those of most other people: his are not "normal" desires but rather obsessions. This is why he manages to stand out: he is ready to make any sacrifice to achieve the goal he works and lives for, his own goal.

The Wise Salesman passionately desires to accomplish his goal, so much so that he is completely enslaved by it. And no other "slavery" could turn out more beneficial and miraculous.

The Wise Salesman well knows the difference between a mere aspiration and an intense desire, which takes the form of an obsession. Everybody seeks happiness, money, fame, acknowledgement, or many other forms of "abundance," but most people stop at the phase of mere aspiration, being completely devoid of fundamental action plans. The Wise Salesman, on the contrary, knows exactly what he wants and knows he has a destiny to fulfil. He is determined and does not stop at simple aspiration, but rather is constantly pushing himself to intensify it, transforming it into an obsessive desire that burns inside him night and day.

The Wise Salesman knows that he will need an effective plan and a constant effort to achieve his goal. He does not simply strive. Unlike the unsuccessful, he turns his plans into reality, thanks to a precise strategy.

The Wise Salesman is convinced that nothing can take the place of an ambitious goal. When he clearly and decidedly establishes a definite purpose, the powers of the universe seem to take his side.

The Wise Salesman is a winner because he believes he can win. His faith overcomes every limit. He loves success, and he is sure he will manage to achieve it. He never thinks, "Maybe I want too much." The idea of failure does not occur to him, because he does not like it and he refuses to accept it. His vocabulary does not include words such as "impossible," "failure," "retreat," "give up." Such words are for losers. Every obstacle is nothing but a temporary deviation from the aim. He has a feeling inside that he will surely achieve his goal in the end, and he feels so even before starting his struggle, simply because he believes in the effectiveness of his strategy, unlike the unsuccessful, who fight without really striving for victory.

The Wise Salesman, obsessed with his goal, constantly persists because he knows the value of perseverance, and he strongly believes that his sacrifices will be rewarded one day. He believes that the greatest of all risks in life is never taking any risk. Those who risk nothing do nothing, are nothing, will have nothing. By constantly striving and attacking, the Wise Salesman will succeed. Perseverance always pays back. Just like the river, which overcomes the rock by its perseverance, the Wise Salesman persists so that no power can resist him. However, he never makes the mistake of confusing perseverance with insistence. He knows that some challenges might carry on for longer than necessary, burning up his forces and undermining his enthusiasm. He reflects and remembers these wise words: "Too long a war ends up by destroying the winner too." So he decides to change battlefield, giving up his insistence but persevering with his will until he finds a better customer for a new sale.

On his path to success, the Wise Salesman also receives some unexpected blows. He does realize that he will inevitably lose a few battles: nobody wins all the time. When this happens and he is filled with despair, he initially thinks that nothing will be able to awaken his enthusiasm again. The others comment, "Maybe his fight is over." At this, the Wise Salesman feels sorrow and confusion, because he still could not achieve the goal he was striving for. But he is tenacious and does not give up what he started. Immediately, he takes up the fight for his goal again, because the longer he lingers in desperation, the further his dreams drift away. If a horseman falls from his horse and does not get back up within a minute, he will never have the courage to remount again.

The Wise Salesman can lose and never will minimize his defeats with comments like, "After all, it wasn't that important" or "That wasn't what I really wanted". He accepts his temporary defeat and carries on his path, working hard to prove his value because he knows that at the end of the arid desert he will find fresh, green grass. He gladly leaves the desperation to losers and does not waste his energies on complaints. Words would be useless. He never brings himself down with thoughts like, "I hate losing. I can't stand it." He rather resists and perseveres. Time will turn to his favour again. Prizes are to be found only at the end of the path, never at the start or halfway through. And he has no way of knowing how much time he will need in order to reach the desired goal. It is not the single battle that interests him. What is important is to win the war to conquer his goal.

The Wise Salesman always behaves somewhat out of the ordinary. He likes to stand out—he cannot be like anybody else. He has to distinguish himself. He has written down a detailed description of his goal and reads it aloud, repeating every day what he wishes for, until it becomes a habit. The Wise Salesman can afford such behaviours and does not fear the judgement of other people, because he is ready to stand up for an idea, even if it looks ridiculous or foolish to the masses.

He can also decide not to let others see him while he carries out his daily "ritual," staying on his own, because he is able to use solitude to gain time for himself when necessary.

Repeating the sentences that make up his goal, and imagining or even feeling that he has already accomplished it, the Wise Salesman makes his words become a part of his active mind. They are absorbed by his subconscious, the most mysterious part of his mind, where thoughts work like a "magnet" attracting similar, positive thoughts. Simply reading his goal aloud would not be enough if the Wise Salesman did not enrich his words with faith, emotion, and feeling, convincing himself more and more. It would not be enough, if he did not talk to his own heart. After all, he does not believe in fate and knows that man is responsible for his own destiny. He can master himself and what surrounds him, precisely because of his ability to influence his subconscious through his active mind.

The Wise Salesman knows that success comes, first of all, through a clear and concise mental image of what he wishes for. Mind is also the only thing he can have complete command over. Since he is certain that his thoughts can influence his life, his life begins to change. This positive image of change, nourished by the obsessive desire, seeps in his subconscious, thus making every venture seem possible no matter how exceptional it may be. His subconscious, in effect, builds a bridge between the mental image and its physical equivalent, which automatically attracts the Wise Salesman.

As this attraction gains more and more strength, the Wise Salesman experiences an incredible vitality, never experienced until that moment. He is pervaded by a mysterious force that is able to wipe out fear and procrastination and give him happiness through the burning flame of enthusiasm. The constant repetition of his obsessive desire and of the action strategy related to it bring about a positive thought habit, which makes every action look easier and more pleasant. A deep and burning desire, if kept alive, is absorbed by the subconscious and carried out much more quickly than a "normal" desire. The subconscious remains deaf to normal desires, focusing first of all on those desires that have become usual and dominant.

The Wise Salesman loves his positive habits. This is why he follows them with great devotion and fidelity.

When you wish for something, the whole Universe conspires for you to achieve it.

—PAULO COELHO

Chapter 3

THE INEXORABLE LAW OF CAUSE AND EFFECT: GIVE TO OBTAIN

The Wise Salesman believes that what creates an effect was already there in the cause. This is a law of nature, a just and inexorable law. No matter what initiative one may take up, nobody can escape the law of cause and effect. The Wise Salesman is aware that, in order to achieve his goal, he will have to, in return, provide a useful service as valuable as the goal he strives for. Overlooking this principle leads many to perennial dissatisfaction. Those who delude themselves by thinking they can obtain something in return for nothing (or least for a less valuable service) are condemned to mediocrity.

The Wise Salesman, on the contrary, knows that there is an indissoluble bond, a precise connection, between what one gives and what one obtains. He knows that, to realize his goals, he must create a commensurate cause, a cause that shows up in his daily efforts, his action plans, his passion, his desire, his perseverance and his positive mental attitude. He always gives the best of himself, and this is why he expects the best from life.

The Wise Salesman succeeds because he is ready to assume huge responsibilities and offer a quite exhaustive service, unlike most of his fellow men, who meet failure and defeat because they do not go to as great lengths as he does.

The Wise Salesman has almost no limitations in setting the height of his goal because nobody can prevent him from desiring and determining the value he wants to reach. He is the only one who can do it, deciding the quality and quantity of the services he offers, in addition to the mental attitude he chooses to have while one his path. Once he acknowledges this truth, he comes to realize that there is no injustice in the difference between the goals he deservingly reaches and the failures of many other salesmen. Through the law of compensation, by which all must necessarily abide, it is possible to determine one's relationship with life, including one's success.

The Wise Salesman is convinced that the unsuccessful are such because they are content with the results they have already achieved, without striving for higher goals, mostly because of their self-imposed mental limitations and idleness. They do nothing useful to put the world in a condition to pay back their services. They carry on doing what they have always done, and this is the reason why they will forever be losers.

The Wise Salesman is never overwhelmed by such thoughts as: "There are no opportunities. I won't make it." He never uses the lack of opportunities to justify his defeats. Mediocre people, on the contrary, are oppressed by laziness and have no ambitions. They use this excuse to justify their inability to take up hard tasks and to use their mind to create new opportunities. The Wise Salesman strongly believes that there is no such thing as people born under an unlucky star; if anything, there are people who are unable to look up at the sky properly. And the sky of opportunities is endless. The Wise Salesman has a very broad view; the world of great opportunities is at his feet. The opportunities are hidden, as a matter of fact, in his foresight, his determination, his initiative, and his knowledge. But above all, opportunities are hidden in his consciousness of his own value and in the promotion of his qualities. He knows that the power of the eagle is based on its sharp sight, and that the lion is superior to the gazelle because it is conscious of its greater strength. Therefore, the Wise Salesman tries to figure out what it is he can count on, and he refines his "equipment" with the best of what he has hidden in his heart. Since his heart sees things that are invisible to the eye, the Wise Salesman sees opportunities even where others see nothing.

The Wise Salesman knows the secret to success. He never thinks: "I had such great opportunities. How lucky I am." He does not believe in chance because he knows the source of his luck. All the favourable occasions he profited from were created by him and him alone, thanks to his initiative. He well knows that, if he wishes for more, he must offer a greater service than what he has provided up to that moment. In order to satiate his limitless ambitions, he needs to acquire the best of all habits: the habit of giving more. This is the only way he can harmoniously learn his destiny towards victory and oppose greed, which pushes people to try and obtain things in return for nothing.

The Wise Salesman is aware that life does not always pay him back immediately when he decides to give something more. Sometimes he actually gets nothing. But he never gives in. On the contrary, he stands by this principle, using whatever tools he can. Sooner or later he will be rewarded. He freely chooses to take up this habit because he knows that the mind is a key to success, and he knows how powerful the mind is. The mind tends to infinity and has no limitations, except self-imposed ones. Combining this ability with a positive mental attitude, with faith, with a broad vision, and with the disposition to always give something more, the Wise Salesman can achieve whatever he wants in life. He is free, and this is why he succeeds. He is the master of his own mind, his own emotions, and his own actions. But above all, he is the master of his own destiny because nobody can restrain him. If he simply carried out the duties somebody else imposed on him, if he simply worked the hours he was supposed to, he would barely secure his mere survival. The Wise Salesman, on the contrary, often makes great sacrifices, tries to do more than he has ever done; at the end of the day, he tries hard to drive one more sale, disregarding the successes or the failures of the day, no matter the late hour, without gloating about his victories or wallowing in the sorrow for his defeats. He must always give something more, day by day, to promote himself and finally reach excellence. The days of the Wise Salesman begin early: he does not like to linger in bed. And they end late: he never tries to shorten his working days. On the contrary, he tries to lengthen them. He rushes to work with the same enthusiasm of a starving man rushing towards food. He is always busy: he is a slave to his goal, but he is free in his daily steps.

The Wise Salesman cannot stand comments such as: "Why should I work for more than I am paid for." He knows that those who reason that way are bound to fail because they only work as much as necessary to survive, earning just enough to satisfy their bare necessities. They cannot and must not expect to receive more than they give.

The Wise Salesman knows that giving something more is not just an act of generosity but above all something he carries out for his own interest, because a greater service will pay him back more. Moreover, this beneficial habit attracts to him the favourable attention of people who can offer him opportunities for success. This is how he makes it to victory. After all, nobody is unhappy when he accomplishes more than what he had promised, especially if he has a friendly and open mental attitude capable of inspiring trust in others. He will become indispensable for his customers, and he will be well rewarded.

The Wise Salesman knows the laws of nature and turns them to his benefit, profiting from them. When a seed is planted, nature gives back a tree rich in fruits. Nature never does anything useless. It is a simple yet powerful law, without which life itself could not exist on earth. What use would it be if nature simply gave back the same seed after it were planted? Nature constantly makes more than is expected of it because this is what is needed to secure life on earth. The Wise Salesman is a good sower because he is convinced that his efforts of today will multiply his value of tomorrow, turning the one seed into many ripe fruits. Thanks to his intelligence, to his knowledge, and to the sacrifices he makes in his work, he will get back much more than what he sowed. The seed, before becoming a tree rich in fruits, must face the darkness of the earth it was planted in. Just like the seed, the Wise Salesman must face and defeat the darkness of his fears, his uncertainties, and his failures before finally seeing the bright light of success. And just like the sun must warm up the plant to make it flourish, so the burning desires of the

- Wise Salesman must light up in his spirit the hunger for victory, motivating him to pursue his goal.

The Wise Salesman believes in the impossible, and this is why he does the impossible to accomplish the impossible.

The only true way to success is to provide more and better service than what's expected from you, no matter what the task is.

—OG MANDINO

Chapter 4

THE FAITH TO WIN AND ACHIEVE SUCCESS

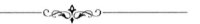

he Wise Salesman is happy if the light of faith shines in his eyes and lights up his heart. He totally and deeply accepts his goal because he firmly believes in the reason he fights for. Then the people praise him, "Your faith is extraordinary!" And he cannot help but be proud of this. Even if he does not want to use his faith to attract the admiration of other people, it shows through their praise.

The Wise Salesman does not need to prove anything to anyone. He never tries to show off. He simply is, because faith lies inside his spirit. It originates in the depth of his thoughts and in the maze of his mind, and it flames up in his heart, is carried forward by the flow of his ardent desire.

The Wise Salesman knows that thoughts are extremely powerful, because as impalpable as they may be, they can still be turned into reality. The realm of thought, as a matter of fact, is the place where every success has its origin and where every desire starts on its path to become reality. The striving for and realization of a plan are nothing but an extension of this thought. Action, therefore, can be regarded as a thought that was given wings. This is why thoughts are things. It is an immutable principle that nourishes faith and underlies every achievement.

When the Wise Salesman focuses on the positive thought that his goal will surely be achieved and when he carries out, at the same time, a well-defined plan, his self-confidence grows exponentially, soaring up high. This mental condition is at his total command and is based on faith. But this faith has nothing to do with supernatural or theological ideas. It is rather an essential power to master one's own mind and be able to soar above mediocrity. It is an irresistible force by which nothing is impossible.

The Wise Salesman voluntarily develops the feeling of faith through the reiteration of the orders he gives to his subconscious, through the repetition of positive thoughts and through autosuggestion, which lead him to be certain that what he wishes for can be achieved. Faith is a magic cloak for him: after enveloping a thought, it magically turns it into its real, tangible thing, allowing dreams to come true.

The faith of the Wise Salesman is never blind, because it is never based on unclear or unplanned actions. Nor is it a mystery, because the Wise Salesman very well knows the extraordinary power of the mind and the best way to use it—unlike unsuccessful salesmen, who have no idea of how to profit from it. The Wise Salesman's only faith stems from facts, from reasonableness, and from clear intentions. He never makes the mistake of those people who accuse him of being inconsistent: "How can you have a faith based only on proven facts? Faith is in the unknown!" But this argument is superficial. The Wise Salesman is not interested in a scientific demonstration of his faith. What he really cares about is to feel it inside him, true and crystal clear, confirmed by every one of his steps towards success. He gazes into the universe and feels that life is sustained by a universal order, a precise plan, thought out by an intelligence infinitely superior to what man can conceive. The perfect organization of the natural laws, the mystery of life showing up in daily miracles, and the ability of man to think, reason, and feel: all these are elements that confirm his faith. Once he assumes this point of view, he is free from any contradiction, maintaining confidence in himself and in his own faith.

The Wise Salesman knows that the mind is the only thing he can have complete command of. The mind is so powerful that conscience was wisely added to it in order to tame its power and use it to solve any existential problem. The Wise Salesman is absolutely certain about one thing: the mind has incredible imagination, which offers him ways and means to make his goal come true. Unlike knowledge, which, as vast as it may be, is always limited, imagination is an infinite universe. This is why it always turns out to be more useful than knowledge for the achievement of success. Moreover, the mind triggers desire and enthusiasm, and above all, it awakens faith.

It is the mind of the Wise Salesman that shapes his personality: it selects, controls, and modifies the nature of his thoughts. Through his mind, the source of all his happiness, the Wise Salesman decides which thoughts to focus on. This way he can concentrate all his energies on the activities that are controlled by the power of his thought. "If you can imagine it, you can do it." The Wise Salesman is fascinated by the dreamers who managed to achieve success. The mind has no reasonable limits except self-imposed ones deriving from a lack of faith. It is the bridge of faith that connects the end of the imagination with that of the realization of one's goal. Without faith, no wish could ever come true.

Faith is not the exclusive property of the Wise Salesman. It has no copyright. Anybody can possess it since it is a universal power within everybody's reach, from the humblest to the wealthiest. Anybody, at any moment, can learn faith. It is not an innate quality endowed at birth upon a few people only. Moreover, the

Wise Salesman is well aware that some people are slaves to fears and hardships that are not really there in their life but are simply imaginary and not at all necessary. The only thing to fear is fear itself. This is why the Wise Salesman is convinced that fear is the greatest of all mankind's obstacles. He knows that everybody is afraid of everybody and that many people have had to face the same obstacles he did and share the same uncertainties as he had. But unlike others, the Wise Salesman has overcome his limitations, using fear as an engine and not as a brake. By cleverly using his mind, he has acquired faith, because he has finally got rid of the ghosts of his enemies: negative thoughts and self-imposed limitations. The void left by the disappearance of such enemies was naturally filled up by faith, that extraordinary positive power able to wipe away all fears and destroy, one after the other, all obstacles that life presents him with.

The Wise Salesman reckons that many fears can be easily overcome because they are imaginary. People fear poverty, although they are surrounded by wealth and the opportunities to reach it. People fear illness, although our body is designed by nature to automatically heal and stay efficient. People fear criticism, although they do not really receive any and it only comes from imaginary critics. People fear losing the love of their loved ones, although they know that the right behaviours can keep love alive and strengthen it for years. People fear old age, although it is an essential key to understanding life, being a source of wisdom and experience. People fear the restriction of freedom, although they know they can preserve it if they maintain a harmonious relationship with society. People fear death, although it is inevitable. People fear failure and are not able to see that every failure carries in itself the seeds of a new success.

With faith, the Wise Salesman overcomes all his fears. And since he believes in his goal, he will achieve it.

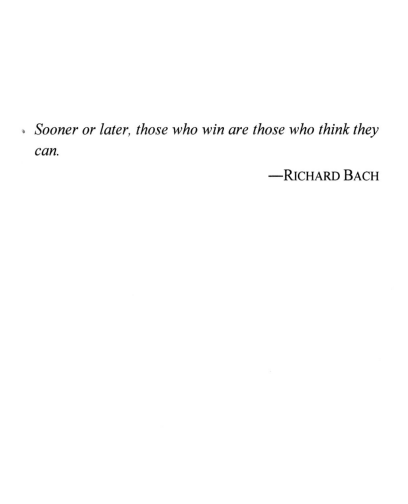

Sooner or later, those who win are those who think they can.

—RICHARD BACH

Chapter 5

HOW TO FACE DEFEAT

On his way to his goal, the Wise Salesman realizes he will inevitably face a few defeats. He decides to equip himself the best he can and starts to look for the perfect "armour." For this purpose, he listens to the suggestions of other salesmen: "Use the shield of cynicism," says one. "Wear the armour of craftiness," whispers another. "The best armour is to always think about your own interests," adds a third one. The Wise Salesman, though, refuses all these suggestions. With happiness in his heart, he wears the indestructible cloak of faith, which will help him parry all blows and turn failures into victories. His success depends on his ability to get back up after defeats. This ability will allow him to develop strength and wisdom, to make failures something accidental and successes something permanent.

The Wise Salesman, though, is not always animated and fired up by faith. He does have moments of despair, when his failures make him lose confidence. In those moments, he is attacked by doubts and asks his heart: "Is it still worth making the sacrifices and fighting?" But his heart is silent and he has to decide by himself. Then he goes looking for examples, and sees how successful people, although sometimes crushed under the weight of defeat, never gave up their fight and heroically faced their unfavourable situation. Still unable to find his faith again, the Wise Salesman decides to persevere, because however far away his goal may be, there is always a way to overcome obstacles. And faith, eventually, comes back. After all, he can always count on the indestructible cloak of faith, which envelops him even when the light in his eyes seems to be fading.

When faith shows up again in the soul of the Wise Salesman, his beliefs get stronger, pushed forward by the renewed and unrestrained force of fresh motivation. He will try and try again in the face of every difficulty because he knows that every problem is actually a hidden opportunity, that every failure will increase his possibilities of success the next time, that for every defeat he will achieve a victory, that every "no" he hears brings him closer to the long-desired sound of "yes," that every tear he sheds prepares him for a future smile, that the bad luck of today contains the seeds of the good luck of tomorrow, that the poverty he suffers will make him appreciate his future richness more, that the darkness of the night is necessary to love the light of the sun, that he must first feel anger to learn the value of peace, that he must first learn silence to learn the weight of words, and that he may have to fail many time to succeed just once. All those who have faith know this. All those who have faith look beyond appearances.

The Wise Salesman always has a positive mental attitude, even when he faces failure, because in life, defeats are inevitable. He considers them as purely accidental, as occasional episodes, as a gym to train his strength of will, as valuable occasions to test his spirit. He glimpses in defeat a clear and stimulating signal of the need for a change of plans, because it is always possible to take the wrong turn on the way to success. The deviations from his path do cause him some moments of despair. Often he finds himself in situations he already had to face and gets the impression he is not advancing, since his defeats seem to be repeating. He complains in his heart, "I have already lived through this situation." "That is true, but you have not yet overcome it," replies his heart. Then he realizes that the repetition of his defeats has but one purpose: to teach him a different way to success.

Being extremely self-confident, the Wise Salesman never allows one defeat to stop him. After all, he knows that if he lost confidence in himself, the whole universe would turn against him. Optimism prevails over his momentary discouragement. In those moments, he thinks, "There are no insurmountable problems!" Therefore, he accepts a change of plan, without changing his goal. The power of his determination stays untouched in any circumstance, no matter the difficulties of the way, because he will not allow anything or anybody to snuff out his burning desire to win. Once he has started on his path to success, he goes all the way and does not allow hardships to scare him away, because he is aware that, without his goal, he would be nothing.

The Wise Salesman knows that the best way to prevent failure is an easy yet effective technique: he accustoms his mind to take defeats into account in advance. Failure, just like success, is first of all a psychological condition deriving from habit. Thanks to this technique, he develops a positive habit, allowing him to fully master his own mind and to use it to turn failures into opportunities. Self-discipline helps him turn unpleasant emotions into a driving power, train his strength of will, and activate his subconscious in a positive way. The Wise Salesman pays a great deal of attention to habits. He knows that both failure and victory are first of all mental conditions. He can meet victory if he develops a plan to attain it, but he can also meet defeat if he lacks a precise plan. The subconscious acts according to its dominant mental attitude. This is why he tries to consolidate his positive habits through his goal, his plans to achieve it, and his subconscious. The mind, if used the right way, constitutes a starting point to success and offers solutions to problems as they show up. The Wise Salesman, learning how to use his mind, becomes free, unlike the unsuccessful, who are prisoners in the jail of their self-imposed limitations and completely resigned to defeat.

The Wise Salesman always sees a positive side in every defeat. He is incurably optimistic and accustoms his subconscious to transform negative experiences into a stimulating drive to realize more ambitious enterprises. Whenever he rises from defeat, he takes great mental and spiritual advantages of it, gaining strength and discovering his true essence. He has suffered, yes, but he has surely learned never to make the same mistakes again.

Whenever he loses, the Wise Salesman wishes for victory even more ardently than before, and this is why he will eventually achieve it.

The art of winning is learned in defeat.

—SIMÓN BOLÍVAR

Chapter 6

HOW TO WIN THE TRUST OF OTHERS

The Wise Salesman pays a great deal of attention to the way children look at things because their eyes can see the world without bitterness. When he wishes to know whether others trust him or not, he tries to understand how a child would look at him. He needs to feel appreciated and appear trustworthy in the eyes of other people. When he notices that somebody mistrusts him, doubts assail him: "Am I not behaving the way I should?" Then he remembers that the art of sales is based on the ability to develop an attractive personality, capable of inspiring trust. The Wise Salesman has a dignity to maintain. This is why he appreciates the value of honesty. He knows very well that those who do not keep their word lose the respect of others as well as their self-respect. He has seen many salesmen feel ashamed of their actions. Their life always consists of a humiliating retreat. They surely have wasted more energy in fleeing than in trying to keep their word. He has often seen salesmen behave in the wrong way, cheating innocent customers who later turned against others who were weaker than them out of anger and cowardice. These, in their turn, take revenge on others, starting a chain of unhappiness. Nobody can guess the consequences of their actions, and this is why the Wise Salesman always behaves honestly and accepts only customers who are worthy of him.

The Wise Salesman wins the trust of other people because he shows he deserves it, through loyal, honest, and reliable conduct, providing his customers with the same service he would wish for himself. He never lies nor "conceals" anything about his business, avoiding pointless and dangerous risks that could jeopardize his success. He knows that the best of all salesmen is the one who tells the truth, because no matter the outcome of the bargain, he will leave a great impression on his customers. And anyways, not many people are fooled by beautiful words that aren't followed by facts. Time after time, a dishonest salesman will end up fooling not only others but himself too. Therefore, the Wise Salesman achieves success not because he is the most eloquent but simply the most sincere. Sincerity, as a matter of fact, is the main quality that helps him win the trust of other people.

The Wise Salesman also knows that success is rewarded to those who know their business well. A prepared salesman inspires more trust and gains more approval. He never misses an occasion to learn. No matter the age, whoever carries on learning is young, while whoever stops learning is old. Therefore, he constantly tries to improve, deepening his knowledge about himself, about mankind, and about the wares he sells, so as to multiply his chances of success.

The Wise Salesman knows that it is not up to him to judge others. He does not waste time and energy criticizing the behaviour of other people. He never looks for occasions to gossip. He does not need to prove that others are wrong to believe in his success. He remembers the words of Benjamin Franklin: "Never speak badly about anyone, always commend everyone the best that you can." His behaviour is loyal, and he praises his competitors when they deserve it. He even commends his enemies, making them into his friends. Such behaviour will make his personality notably more respectable.

The Wise Salesman is never a prey to envy, one of the great parasites of the human spirit, a carrier of evil. He cannot prevent others from envying him, but he can surely oppose envy by refusing to be envious himself. He knows that envy would devour all his energy, which he needs to reach his desired goal and without which he would turn into a simple spectator of the success of others. Instead, he tries to reach excellence. He focuses on his abilities and convinces himself he is the greatest miracle of nature. He starts by promoting his qualities and his virtues, being aware of his uniqueness. He feels like an inimitable work of art, impossible for others to copy because the brush strokes of his success are unique and pure genius. He stops imitating others and shows his own distinctive abilities instead. He displays before the whole word his peculiarities, hiding his most common traits. Proud of his distinctiveness, he becomes aware that he is not on this earth by chance. On the contrary, he has a definite purpose: his goal, his unique and valuable goal. Although he is a salesman, what satisfies others is not enough for him.

Inside the Wise Salesman a flame burns that has been passed down through countless generations, just like the profound words of Robert Rudolf Schmidt suggest: "When one leans down to gaze into the darkness of the primordial ideas and beliefs, one hears the voice of blood, because the spirit of prehistoric times is alive in each one of us. These necessary steps of thought are what make up the life of our subconscious. Every generation, in a fatal chain of actions, passes down to the next one this primordial torch." The flame of this torch constantly stimulates his spirit to become better than what it is. And he will surely improve, feeding the fire of his restlessness and proclaiming to the world his uniqueness.

The Wise Salesman counts on the quality of his actions, which are always honest and crystal clear, to inspire trust in the other people. He is never afraid they might complain about him because he is sure he always behaves properly. Through such a modus operandi, he ensures himself favourable testimonies and enthusiastic friends, who cannot but speak well of him, enhancing enormously his credibility. The Wise Salesman never praises himself. He lets others do that for him.

The Wise Salesman does not hesitate to talk about his successes and the strategies he adopted. His friends comment: "Why would you reveal your plans like this? Don't you see that this way you might have to share your victories with somebody else?" But he just smiles without answering. He knows that if he reached an empty paradise after achieving his goal, his fight would have been pointless. He needs to feel appreciated and surrounded by the favour of the other people, and he knows that the only way to conquer pettiness and subterfuge is to speak open-heartedly. Like all open and transparent people, he always dares to confront and interact directly with others, but he never makes the mistake of talking about his dreams before realizing them.

The Wise Salesman is always trustworthy, and this is how he manages to win everybody's esteem.

In all things, the trust one inspires constitutes half of the success. The trust one feels is the other half.

—VICTOR HUGO

Chapter 7

THE CHARACTERISTICS OF A
WINNING PERSONALITY

he Wise Salesman always tries to improve his personality, developing a series
of characteristics that make him look
more amiable and pleasant. He knows that a charming
personality is like a perfume that everybody is attracted
to. He knows the power of KINDNESS and does not
hesitate to dedicate time to it, in his daily contact with
others. His kind behaviour turns into a constant habit of
respecting and helping others without any egoism. This
attitude opens up many unexpected opportunities for
him.

The foundation of the Wise Salesman's personality
is his mental attitude. He knows that a negative mental

attitude would make him enemies and lead to a loss of customers. He would be defeated even before starting his fight, disregarding all other factors. On the contrary, a POSITIVE MENTAL ATTITUDE towards himself and others attracts success, modifying his thoughts and their way of manifesting themselves, with positive consequences for the people who surround him. It is not an innate quality. He developed it with great effort by growing accustomed to express it and keep it alive day by day.

The Wise Salesman is LOVING, because without love he would be nothing. He knows that one of the secrets of success in any human activity is to face life with a heart full of love. Brute force can destroy any obstacle, but only the invisible power of love can open up people's hearts. Gathering love leads to good fortune, while gathering hate leads to calamity. Therefore, the Wise Salesman sharpens the sword of his love and defeats evil, crushing the walls of hate and anger. He does not have time to hate, only to love. People may distrust his words, look at him with suspicion, and be wary of his propositions, but the warmth of his love will melt the frozen hearts of many. For the Wise Salesman, to face the path to his goal with love means to feel everything with love. It means to love the sun because it warms him up but also to love the rain because it purifies his spirit. It means to love the light because it lights his way but also to love the darkness because it allows him to see the stars. It means to welcome victories because he deserves them but also to accept obstacles because they are his challenge. To face life with love means to treat people with love. The Wise Salesman encourages his friends to always try to find a reason to commend them. He is able to rejoice in their success as if it were his own, and this is how his friends become like brothers to him. This is how he faces every person on his way. Who can tell him no while feeling the love in his heart? The power of love unites and helps him advance towards success. On the path to his goal, the Wise Salesman is ready to love anybody, provided that they deserve admiration and above all are worthy of his love. Sadly, in the past, he did have to deal with people who did not deserve his love. But the winners do not repeat the same mistake twice, and this is why he puts his heart at stake only if it is really worth it. He loves the ambitious because they inspire him; he loves the unsuccessful because they can help him understand the mistakes to avoid. He loves the kings because they are nothing but men; he loves the king's subjects because they are divine. He loves the rich because they are lonely; he loves the poor, because they are a multitude. He loves the young for their dreams; he loves the old for their wisdom. And above all, the Wise Salesman loves himself. He does anything he can to be better. He takes care of his body as well as his mind. He does not allow his body to indulge too much in the most ephemeral pleasures and his mind to be tempted too much by sin. He knows how dangerous bad habits are and refuses to become their slave. He loves himself too much to let himself succumb to self-destruction.

The Wise Salesman is FLEXIBLE: he can adapt to any circumstances and to sudden changes without losing his inner balance. He easily finds a harmony with the environment around him thanks to a remarkable personal ability to adapt, which helps him face, in the best way possible, the constant and inevitable changes of life conditions and human relationships. The Wise Salesman behaves like water, flowing among the obstacles he encounters on his way to success. He knows that he cannot directly oppose all situations because there are moments when not adapting would lead to his complete destruction. Therefore, without complaining, he lets the obstacles trace his route.

This is what the force of water is all about: It cannot be crushed by a hammer or pierced by a sword. Not even the most powerful of weapons can damage it, let alone leave a scar on its cloak. The water of a river adapts to its course, without ever losing sight its destination—the sea. Although very fragile at its spring, the river gets stronger as it flows towards its goal, gaining strength from the rivers it meets on its course. After some time, its power becomes unrestrained: the achievement of its goal is now inevitable.

When the Wise Salesman sets out his goal, he is sincere. The SINCERITY OF THE GOAL is a distinctive and fundamental trait of his character, allowing him to stay true and never modify the reality of facts. Concealing the nature of his goals is something that does not belong to his way of action. This is how he always manages to let his force show in every word he utters, in the expression of his face, in his tone of voice, in the service he provides with his work, and in many other less visible ways connected with feelings. The Wise Salesman never says, "Yes, sir!" He is too sincere to be this insincere, and anyway no act of sincerity, if sustained by a positive and constructive intention, can ever be regarded as an act of insubordination.

The Wise Salesman knows that opportunities, however numerous they may be, never wait for anybody. Only a vision able to see opportunities where others see impossibility, only the right READINESS OF DECISION, allows him to catch favourable occasions and to advance. Unlike him, the unsuccessful hesitate and falter, unable to decide. In a fast-changing world, only those who are quick at deciding can win. The Wise Salesman makes a habit of deciding quickly and ardently focusing on his goal. He does not follow anybody's recipes, formulas, or tricks. He considers every situation as if it were unique and always tries to act at the right moment.

The Wise Salesman is RELIABLE because he is always able to accomplish whatever he promises. When he talks, he shows a bit of what he thinks and tries hard to live up to the ideas he publicly defends, because it is his credibility that is at stake. When he is in doubt, he keeps silent, avoiding exposing himself. Because he believes he is what he says, he ends up by becoming who he says he is.

The Wise Salesman never lets negative feelings get hold of him. He knows and appreciates one of the greatest gifts life has for us: the ability to LAUGH at the world. With a smile, he paints his days on a canvas of happiness. He laughs in front of good, and good multiplies. He laughs in front of evil, and evil disappears. This habit is incredibly healthy for both the body and the spirit. It lightens the burden of defeat and makes the way to success easier and more pleasant. He knows he is nothing before the immensity of the world and the unfathomable mystery of life. This is why he faces his days with a smile to make them become merrier, turning the sources of sadness to nothing. If one day he is crushed by defeat, he smiles, knowing that it will pass. If one day he is exalted by success, he just laughs, because he knows that even that will pass. He laughs at the world with happiness in his heart, so as to make every day into a triumph. All of this also turns to his benefit because he knows that no one buys from a sulking salesman and tears have no value on the market. Every smile, on the contrary, is worth gold and pays him back for his sacrifices. The Wise Salesman never takes himself too seriously. He laughs at himself too because he knows that men become ridiculous when they are too austere, cold, and distant. He has a marked sense of humour, which helps him be flexible and adapt to the variable circumstances of life. The Wise Salesman laughs at the world, and this is why he will be happy and surely succeed.

The Wise Salesman is TOLERANT and never judges others on the basis of concepts like "right" and "wrong." He rather judges on the basis of the most fitting behaviour for a situation. He knows that everybody, in life, will have to adapt to different circumstances sooner or later: he is not surprised to see people change their attitude. He always gives everybody the time and occasion to explain the reasons for their actions and change, since he is open-minded and always ready to accept new points of view. He is never limited in his quest for knowledge, and this is why, in his mind, he is constantly growing.

The Wise Salesman knows that there is always an appropriate and an inappropriate moment to do things, and this is why he pays great attention to what he says and what he does. He is always quite TACTFUL, because he has grown accustomed to being very sensitive in interacting with others.

The Wise Salesman believes that one of the greatest rewards in life is to deserve the trust of others, always acting with great intellectual integrity and a deep SENSE OF JUSTICE. He distrusts those who act honest just for their convenience because such honesty is too flexible and easy to turn into dishonesty when convenient. His sense of justice is rooted so deeply in his conscience that it would be impossible for him to see injustice without reacting. He knows that all is one and that every single action may affect all the people on the planet through the foolish chain of unhappiness. Therefore, when he finds himself confronted with the unhappiness of other people, he does not hesitate to fight to help them. This way, he attracts friends and drives away enemies, shielding himself from the destructiveness of controversies. But injustice does happen in life, and even the Wise Salesman is sometimes forced to suffer it. When he finds himself involved in a situation he does not deserve, he perseveres and keeps fighting, because his faith is indestructible and whispers to him that sooner or later everything will turn in his favour again. Digging in his past, he finds out that he is not the only one to have suffered from injustice, and sometimes he has even committed it himself. Nobody is perfect. Nobody can honestly boast and say, "I always behaved correctly." Whoever says so is a liar or does not know himself yet. But the Wise Salesman can make up for his mistakes and make others forgive him, because he always has a second chance. When he meets the people he has wronged, he never misses the valuable occasion to fix the wrong he did. He never hesitates, because in the meantime, he has discovered his goal and developed a deep sense of justice.

The Wise Salesman knows the power of EMOTIONS and knows that they are much harder to govern than reason. He has seen many people fail and fall into the abyss of mediocrity, dragged down by negative emotions. Vice versa, he has also seen people reach the highest peaks of success, gently pushed upwards by positive emotions. The Wise Salesman can control emotions thanks to his mental attitude, since emotions are nothing but psychological conditions, and as such, they are subject to his discipline. With the power of his mind, he can exert control over emotions too. If he could not master his mind, he would risk exposing himself to negative emotions. He knows that if he brought his customers rain, sadness, depression, and pessimism, they would react with rain, sadness, depression, and pessimism, and they would buy nothing. On the contrary, by controlling his mind, he can expose himself to positive emotions. If he brings his customers sun, enthusiasm, joy, and optimism, they react with sun, enthusiasm, joy, and optimism and buy whatever he has to offer. The Wise Salesman is the master of his destiny and cannot let emotionality trouble him. He knows the emotions of the human spirit. There are fourteen, of which seven are positive and seven are negative. The ones that lead to success are love, sublimation, hope, faith, desire, optimism, and loyalty. The negative ones leading to failure are fear, jealousy, hate (which includes envy), vindictiveness, greed, superstition, and wrath. The Wise Salesman plays the melody of his soul combining the notes of emotions on the score of life, using only the positive chords of happiness and success. He knows this art because he got rid of the emotional remains produced in the workshop of his thought. They consist of all the sorrow of his past and have become useless as time has gone by. They consist of careful actions that came to lose their meaning and of memories that, although important, are of no use now. The Wise Salesman has changed his life and started on a new road. He cannot feel anymore what he felt before. And he separates what is useful from what is now unnecessary, keeping the positive emotions and abandoning the useless ones.

The Wise Salesman is always COMPREHENSIVE and never preclusive. He has learned how to control his emotions, and this is why he is patient with everybody, including the angriest and most irritated of his customers, because unlike him, they do not know the secret to control their mind and consequently their emotions. He tolerates insults and cutting remarks because he admits that people can have mood swings, and he is convinced it would be wonderful to meet these people on another occasion when they had the sun in their heart and were more prone to listen to him. He never judges a customer by the first meeting and always sees to it to visit a customer more than once, even if at the beginning the customer seemed hostile. Today he will buy nothing, but tomorrow he might be ready to buy everything. Being aware of this secret helps the Wise Salesman achieve his goal.

The Wise Salesman always shows some INTEREST in people, things, and places and is very versatile. He could not be so attractive if he were unable to concentrate his interest on a topic or a person and maintain it up until the achievement of his objective. The general comprehension of the world he lives in and of human nature is the key to his success. He knows that it is extremely important to listen. Often it turns out to be more important than talking. This is why he pays attention to others: he knows that there is no sweeter compliment, for one who says or does something, than receiving the sincere interest of other people. Vice versa, he knows that there is no ruder insult than interrupting somebody while they are talking or getting distracted and not listening, thus showing one's lack of interest. Thanks to a genuine interest in other people, the Wise Salesman acquires new knowledge over time, observing the details of the virtues and vices of his fellow men. What he learns helps him improve, because the world is a mirror giving back to everyone the reflection of their behaviour. Since he deeply knows himself, he has no difficulty in getting to know others properly. The Wise Salesman has a real passion for people and shows his gratitude without hesitation. People can recognize those who love them and distrust those who do not show as much sensitivity. They recognize them not only based on the words they say but also based on their mental attitudes, which inevitably shape their behaviours, showing at times appreciation and at times contempt. Whoever does not love will not be loved. The heart of the Wise Salesman does not know hate, and he always remembers the words of Jesus, "Love your enemies." And he obeys, although he does not accept everything.

In cases of betrayal, for example, he turns intolerant and merciless because he knows that if he kept too quiet he would lose sight of the horizon of his dreams and drift far from his goal.

The Wise Salesman has a HUMBLE heart and does not know egocentrism, egoism, arrogance, or greed. He is well aware that even the greatest man on earth is nothing before the infinite mystery of life. A humble heart, therefore, is but the consciousness of the unfathomable boundary between man and existence.

The Wise Salesman warmly induces others to cooperate with him, because of his SPORTSMANSHIP. He can achieve success without being too proud, because he never overestimates his victories. In the same way, he can face defeats without whining, avoiding pointless and unproductive comments. This mental attitude, once it has been turned into a habit, secures him the admiration of others and contributes considerably to the attractiveness of his personality.

The Wise Salesman is INTUITIVE. On the way to the realization of his goal, he sometimes faces unforeseen situations. In those moments, he cannot wait and think a strategy over because his destiny will be decided very quickly. He then relies on his intuition, even if this might look like madness, because it is not always possible to follow logic. He is well aware that intuition is the strength of winners, and he carries on writing his success on the parchment of life.

* The Wise Salesman is ATTENTIVE TO DETAILS. He knows that big problems are just a sum of many small mistakes. In order to prevent great catastrophes, he decides to pay the greatest attention to small things, minute after minute. Even after winning many battles, he never lowers his guard on his way to success. He remembers the wisdom of Lao Tzu: "Even if you have fired a bow and arrow many times, continue to pay attention to how you place the arrow, and how you draw the bow." To think about small things does not mean to think small. It rather means to wish for excellence without ever overlooking any detail. His goal, as grand as it may be, is made up of many small achievements, just like the sunlight is made up of a million rays.

The Wise Salesman builds his success on the solid foundation of ELOQUENCE. By enriching his language, he achieves great victories. He knows that one masterful speech during a sale could be enough to earn him huge riches. The Wise Salesman knows well the secrets of rhetoric and tries to use brilliant and effective language in order to communicate force, authority, and confidence about all topics he is competent about. Since he believes in what he says, his speech is rich in feeling. Through the techniques of dramatization and emphasis, he charges his words with emotion, projecting his thoughts on the mind of his listener. Another key element to create this emotional charge is enthusiasm, which gives his words an incredible force. It is not easy to resist the enthusiastic eloquence of the Wise Salesman or to keep one's mind deaf to his thoughts. They flame up with the sacred fire of enthusiasm, which is extremely contagious. He knows that the history of mankind has been marked by people who were able to impose themselves on others with the force of their speaking. This is why he tries to cultivate this art with thorough attention, training himself to speak in a convincing way even in ordinary situations. The Wise Salesman not only believes deeply in what he says but is also an expert about the topics he touches. No rhetoric could match the confidence of an orator who is a master of his subject. The Wise Salesman also knows the moment to stop talking. It is just after he has managed to communicate what he wanted. He is never too lengthy, otherwise his listeners would be bored; he is never too concise, otherwise he could not tell his customers all that might interest them. He knows that people can be influenced only by the words they understand. A speech, however polished it may be, would not be enough to earn him approval if his listeners did not understand enough of it. Therefore, he does not hesitate to use simpler, more effective language, perhaps with a few concrete examples, so that it can be understood by everybody, without becoming too informal or colloquial. He tries to always choose the most appropriate word. Moreover, the Wise Salesman always controls the tone of his voice while he talks, using it to convey specific meanings. The habit of controlling his voice, his means to express emotions, is the key to communicate all his feelings. When he talks to a customer he knows that it is best to use low tones. High tones sound disagreeable and offensive, just like an instrument out of tune breaking the harmony of a melody.

The Wise Salesman pays great attention not only to his verbal language but also to his body language, expressed through GESTURES. He knows that gestures are capable of increasing or undermining the effectiveness of a speech, and therefore, he tends to harmonize them with the context he is in.

Finally, the Wise Salesman also very carefully controls his FACIAL EXPRESSIONS, because the expressiveness of a person tells many things about his character and the feelings he intends to transmit. When he stands before a customer, he intuits what the latter thinks simply by looking into his eyes, because the face, through its expressions, can communicate thoughts and states of mind.

The Wise Salesman has a magnetic personality, and this is why he inevitably attracts success.

You are not what you had previously decided to be, but what you choose to be today.

—WAYNE DYER

Chapter 8

THE DISCIPLINE OF SUCCESS THROUGH ORGANIZED PERSONAL INITIATIVE

The Wise Salesman is convinced that discipline is the ideal bridge between a goal and its realization. No great achievement would be possible without an organized effort. He is perfectly aware of having a great privilege: the opportunity to act by his own initiative. He knows that, without such a privilege, he could never promote himself to realize his dreams. And not only that, for the Wise Salesman, this is not just a right but also a responsibility. He has a destiny to accomplish: the achievement of his goal.

The Wise Salesman regards the right to personal initiative as a privilege because it is something that can raise a man up from mediocrity and failure, leading him to the top of the mountain of success. But he knows that no privilege can produce any benefits unless it is organized and activated by a well-defined plan. If properly organized and done with discipline, this privilege represents a way to realize one's plans, aims, and goals, an engine to turn ideas and ambitions into actual results. If a plan turned out to be weak, it could always be modified. And there is no doubt that any plan is better than procrastination. As a matter of fact, the secret to advance is simply to start! One of the great evils of the world is the detrimental habit of always waiting for the "right moment" without ever beginning. This habit causes more failures than all the wrong plans in the world. This is why the Wise Salesman opposes any form of procrastination: it is totally the opposite of the right to carry out one's own initiative, and as such, it is an enemy of mankind, a time killer, and a life destroyer.

The Wise Salesman knows that opinions are like sand in the desert: in most cases, they are unstable. Everyone can have an opinion about anything, but they are mostly unreliable evaluations. This is why the Wise Salesman is not interested in the opinions of others. He knows that if he hesitated, waiting for everybody's opinion first, he would end up by not acting and he would surely fail. Opinions, if given for free and not coming an authoritative source, unlike those one pays for, represent just an impediment to personal initiative. And anyway, as the Wise Salesman well knows, history has often been marked by unjust and dangerous opinions. When Galileo announced that he had invented a tool with which he had discovered new worlds never before seen by human eyes, the omnipresent opinion-givers cried heresy. They even wanted to burn him alive since he had dared to follow his own initiative. Therefore, the Wise Salesman always mistrusts the opinions of other people. When he wishes to set up an action for the accomplishment of his goal, he does not pay attention to the people who try to dissuade him. Sometimes people tell him, "You can't make it." Many people, out of envy or natural pessimism, tend to frustrate the dreams of others, dragging them into the abyss of mediocrity. The world is full of such prophets of misfortune, victims weighed down by their own inferiority complexes, who were never able to follow their own initiative. But he does not care about them. He never seeks the company of those people who, hiding under a cloak of solidarity, only wish to destroy his self-confidence. Seeing his failure, these so-called friends would probably melt into tears, but they would also be happy in the bottom of their heart. So, the Wise Salesman forgets about the opinion of other people and proves his value by going on his way. He strongly believes that the consequences of his actions will sting his enemies like thorns, while smelling like rose petals to his true friends, who will always stand by his side with sincere love, in good and in bad times. When success finally smiles upon him, the world will fill him with glory and treasures, rewarding him for the courage he showed in standing up for the validity of his ideas. The world needs people who dare to take the initiative and gladly pays them back, rewarding them spontaneously.

The Wise Salesman exercises his right to personal initiative by choice, as an expression of his own will. He is a free man, and no chain could prevent him from climbing the peaks of success, since his actions depend only on his own motivations and desires. He is his own master, the undisputed leader of his existence, unlike the unsuccessful, whose lives are just slavery at the service of the dreams of somebody else. In effect, even if nobody is forced to do anything against their will, he can still see the invisible chains that often bind the endless crowds of these "mindless robots." He can see the bars of their prison, even if it has no walls. It is a prison of the mind, enclosing most of mankind, who delude themselves into thinking they are free when they are not. And this is because many people are unable to make profit of the privilege of personal initiative, out of idleness, scarce ambition, and lack of a goal.

The Wise Salesman can use personal initiative because he is disciplined. He can naturally organize his efforts into a well-defined plan. If he procrastinated, wandering about without a precise aim, he would necessarily fail. He knows that the right moment to use one's personal initiative is immediately after taking a final decision about what one wishes to accomplish.

The Wise Salesman knows that opportunities do not run after anybody. It is men who have to run after opportunities. And the best ones are there to be caught only by those who can organize their efforts most effectively. For this reason, it is very important for him to develop his personal initiative according to a disciplined and organized effort. The Wise Salesman knows the secret to reach whatever height he wishes. This valuable secret consists of the following steps: the choice of a well-defined plan, the development of such plan to reach the desired objectives, constant action to realize the plan, the quest for allies to help him follow the plan, and finally, constant initiative. All of this can be referred to as organized personal effort. It is nothing but a well-planned action, by which anybody can attain excellence. The Wise Salesman does not believe in the existence of geniuses. For him, geniuses are people who can apply specific rules and combine them with their intuition to obtain exactly what they desire. Everybody has genius potential, but most of the time they lack the occasion to express their potential. One's genius might show up in the most diverse activities and situations according to one's character and ambitions. When somebody succeeds where many had failed, sometimes he is called a genius. But all he did was follow the impulse of an ardent, obsessive desire. He patiently carried out a precise plan, firmly supported by the wish to follow his personal initiative.

The Wise Salesman knows that it is very important to organize his knowledge. He reckons that an educated person surely is more likely to succeed than an uneducated one, provided that he can apply his education to the achievement of his goals. He never makes the mistake of believing that an organized personal effort may replace a solid knowledge base. He is fully aware that his success depends not only on what he knows but also on how he uses the knowledge he has gathered. Just like personal effort, even knowledge, if not organized, is not worth much. The Wise Salesman has met many people who were living encyclopaedias but were barely able to make a living since they could not put their knowledge to practice. He is convinced that knowledge is something one gathers on his own through the development and the practice of the mind, because school alone is not enough for a complete education. It is rather one's ability to gather the necessary knowledge for the accomplishment of his goal that makes him really educated. Those who know how and where to look for the knowledge they need are surely more "educated" than those who have studied but do not know how to use what they have learned. He cannot stand such comments as: "I couldn't make my fortune because I didn't have a chance to study." He believes that this is just an excuse for many people to rationalize their failure. Those who really want to get an education eventually find the means to do so, one way or another. Those who are lazy and not ambitious use this excuse to justify their defeat. The Wise Salesman knows that many of the successful people did not study that much from books but were still able to gather all the knowledge they needed to make their dreams come true, reaching the highest levels of society. Through orderly and well-organized action and through experience gathered from practice, they eventually achieved success once they mastered their own mind to aim it towards a well-defined goal. This means acting as educated people do. Organized personal effort is indeed a form of education. The Wise Salesman values the university not for the mere degrees one obtains from it (they alone do not ensure one received an education) but rather for the mental discipline university study forces one to acquire. Combining the mental discipline developed during the college years with the practical experience, the Wise Salesman finds himself in the ideal position to acquire the best of all educations: the one necessary to achieve his goal.

The Wise Salesman never commits the mistake of confusing the freedom to take personal initiative with the freedom to change his mind. He knows that if he were free to change his mind too often without keeping his commitments, his "equipment" would be quite disorderly and his conduct would end up by being pretty disorganized. If he were totally free to change his mind, he could not be consistent in the realization of his plans to reach success. He would surely modify his goals, drifting from one desire to another, inevitably bound for failure. This would never happen if he kept focused on a single, well-defined objective, charting the course to his goal. The soul of the Wise Salesman is free because he can promote himself and soar up to the level he desires. But when he gets really involved in his dreams, then he must wake up at hours he does not like, talk to people who are of no interest to him, carry out menial activities, and make sacrifices. So others say, "You are not free!" But the Wise Salesman is indeed free. He simply knows that an open oven does not bake buns. He freely chose to take this path to success. He knows what awaits him. He freely chose this battlefield. Whatever looks like a restriction on his freedom to others looks like a way to accomplish his goals to him. It is the price to pay for excellence. The Wise Salesman never allows himself to be troubled by those people who preach renouncement just because they are unable to attain ambitious goals.

What I must do is all that concerns me, not what the people think. This rule, equally arduous in actual and in intellectual life, may serve for the whole distinction between greatness and meanness.

—RALPH WALDO EMERSON

Chapter 9

THE GREAT POWER OF ALLIANCES

The Wise Salesman knows the importance of alliances. Even if his is a personal initiative, on his way he can still decide to enjoy the cooperation of other people. working in perfect harmony with other similar minds in order to accomplish a well-defined goal, his own goal. He knows that nobody forces him to make alliances and that he could go on his way alone. but in that case, success would hardly smile upon him. He would be a salesman like any other but not a great salesman, because no single mind can be complete on its own. No single mind can really contain all the knowledge necessary for great accomplishments. Instead, the combination of the education. experience. and ability of many minds constitutes a great treasure of knowledge. It unchains an impalpable and yet beneficial force that no mind alone could ever experience. If the Wise Salesman did not join forces with the others in a spirit of harmony, his accomplishments would surely be humble and mediocre. The lack of comprehension of the importance of the alliances is often the cause of the failure of many. They are unable to recognize the richness of the mind in its broadest sense. It is an immense richness, deriving from the harmonious cooperation of people who work together for the realization of a specific objective.

The Wise Salesman, therefore, is aware that defining a goal is not sufficient to accomplishing it. In order to soar above mediocrity, he needs to contact other people, to enjoy the contribution of their minds in a spirit of perfect harmony. It is essential to have a strong union of purpose and a true, deeply felt union. The Wise Salesman knows that a fake, apparent union would be of no use. It is not enough to put many minds together for them to accomplish a certain goal. Apparent cooperation is totally useless. It is the mental attitude of every single member of the alliance that counts and that can make the difference. A winning alliance consists of a group of people whose minds and hearts are perfectly synchronized with their companions and their leader—that is to say, the one who promoted the alliance.

The Wise Salesman knows the secret to induce other people to cooperate with him in perfect harmony: all men are pushed by their motivation and their habits when they do something. Initially, it is motivation that pushes people towards action, and then it is renewed motivation together with freshly acquired habit that makes them continue, up to the point when they forget their motivation and carry on out of mere habit. And in that case, they fail. Therefore, the Wise Salesman knows that it is essential to select people who are first of all animated by a specific and strong motivation. It must push them to cooperate and resist the passing of time. Another criterion for the selection, of course, is their capability to accomplish what he requires from them. Only a combination of motivation and capability leads to a winning alliance.

The Wise Salesman knows which motivations induce people to join an alliance and remain in it in a spirit of harmony. Such motivations are related to specific emotions that can light up their spirits, such as love, sublimation, the desire for financial gain, the desire for self-preservation, and the desire for self-expression, meaning the desire to receive fame and appreciation from society. Sometimes even negative emotions, like fear and anger, can push one to action. Of all emotions, though, the most powerful for harmonious cooperation are love, sublimation, and desire for financial gain. Of course, it is no absolute principle, since there are people who wish for the acknowledgement of their society more than for material financial gain. The Wise Salesman, in particular, is driven above all by love and sublimation. He tends to success because he knows that to linger in laziness and idleness would cause the unhappiness of his beloved ones, depriving them of all moral and material satisfactions. Through sublimation, his most instinctive and primordial impulses, specifically sexual ones, are directed to non-sexual, elevated goals, and namely to his professional and social success. It is an incredibly powerful energy, able to turn an impulse into a sublimated activity. It turns the primordial aggressiveness to superior, socially accepted levels, constituting the basis for every great economic and intellectual accomplishment.

When the Wise Salesman accomplishes a victory thanks to the help of his allies, somebody comments: "How can he always find people ready to follow him? How lucky he is!" But the Wise Salesman is not lucky. He simply learned to observe people very carefully and can now understand some aspects of them from a first impression. Of course, it is not always easy to judge a person at first sight, but there are certain visible signs that suggest their abilities, and above all, their mental attitude makes all the difference. Those who have a negative mental attitude towards themselves and others tend to be self-centred, egocentric, and pointlessly argumentative. They are not fit for a winning alliance. They are of no benefit for the group and can even become an obstacle that negatively influences the other members of the alliance, frustrating their contribution. And when the harmony of a group is broken, no matter the cause, its ruin is around the corner. The Wise Salesman has seen many salesmen fail because they were unable to understand the key role the harmony and union of purpose played among the members of their team. On the contrary, with a positive and open mental attitude, anybody can recognize the value of harmony and of joint efforts, gaining importance inside the group itself and reaching the top of the hierarchy of success. These are the people the Wise Salesman counts on, because he knows that the combination of efficiency and positive mental attitude is an unbeatable weapon.

The Wise Salesman knows the laws of nature and knows that even the principle of harmonious alliances is part of nature. It was evidently not created by humans, and this can be easily observed. The cooperation of bees, which fervently work all their life for a definite purpose, for the sake of their beehive, is a fitting example to prove how this principle belongs to the great system of the immutable laws of nature. It is also a good example to explain clearly and unmistakably the definition of a goal, so that cooperation may result in success. An important element is the choice of the members of the alliance: they must be completely in tune with the objective. Bees join their forces because they belong to the same species and naturally tend to the same goal. Another key element for the success of an alliance is hard work. Without zeal in their work, bees would never achieve that marvelous stage of cooperation. A group, in order to be productive, must be efficient, active, and zealous. It must work on a well-defined plan, with well-defined timing and a well-defined goal. No matter the type of activity, success requires resolution and organization. As fundamental as the union of the minds may be, it is not enough to make an alliance successful if indecision, idleness, and delay dominate. The Wise Salesman always keeps in mind this proverb: "To prevent a mule from kicking, keep it so occupied it won't have time or desire to kick." A key element to build a winning alliance is motivation. The Wise Salesman has no right, and probably no way, to induce others to cooperate with him if he does not reward them for the service they offer. People do nothing without a motivation, which is therefore the foundation of every alliance. The motivation may be of similar or superior value to that of the required service. The Wise Salesman knows that if he were unable to pay back his allies with a profit similar or superior to their contribution, he would most certainly fail. So he must give them motivation, to convince them to lend him their experience, their knowledge, and their help. Even this is part of the laws of nature. Coming back to the example of bees, when they land on a flower, they establish a symbiotic relationship with it. It is a harmonious alliance, an exchange aimed at the reproduction of the hosting plant and at the "refuelling" of the bee. The latter receives nectar and pollen to share with its colony, while the former receives a small quantity of pollen from flowers of its own species. This kind of an association allows flowers to reproduce and bees to survive. The Wise

Salesman knows that nature is full of harmonious and winning alliances, and this is why he imitates them.

When the Wise Salesman organizes a group who follow his initiative, he must not simply gather it, he must also assume its leadership. As a leader, he has to set the example for all the members of his alliance. He is always in the front line and must try to work harder than any other so as to become indispensable to his allies thanks to his intense effort. He dances with others but assumes every responsibility for his steps. He feels he is at the service of his allies because he thinks nothing is more beautiful than a team of people working together in perfect harmony, each of them focusing on what they can do for the common good. This is why he sincerely hopes his allies will make the most of the alliance. He never stops trying to develop the potential of his team, by whatever means possible. With generosity, he helps everybody show their potential. Some of his collaborators comment, "These are ungrateful people." But he does not let this discourage him. He knows it is important to trust others and not be scared of disappointment. He keeps encouraging his teammates, thus encouraging himself too. He pushes them to accomplish what they desire and yet do not attempt for lack of courage. He knows that the world is full of depressed areas, and that they often imprison the hearts of people so that even just one kind word could help them find the motivation they have lost. Sometimes people blame him: "Who do you think you are, giving advice to everybody? Think about your own defects." The Wise Salesman does know his defects, but he also knows that helping others will earn him their fidelity in return. Being aware that he cannot improve on his own and he cannot advance without allies, he keeps encouraging those who surround him, because he needs faithful companions.

The Wise Salesman is fond of the following proverb: "The best way to tell the world what one wants to do is to show the world what one has already done." This is why the relationship with his allies is always confidential. The goal of a team should never be discussed outside the team itself, unless they are providing a public service. The Wise Salesman never makes the mistake of announcing his goals before he has actually accomplished them. He believes in these words: "Every great man bears in mind a goal which is known only to himself and his God."

The Wise Salesman knows that no one can accomplish great deeds in life without the support of friends. Friends will always prove useful, provided that the feeling between them is mutual, in order not to fall into egoism. He is well aware that he must give to obtain. This is the only way he can expect gratitude. When he builds up an alliance, he always takes care to consolidate friendships with his companions: those who share his goal can be his best masters. When he needs advice, he does not ask far away, unreachable counsellors, but rather those who stand closest to him. He tries to observe how his friends solve, or do not solve, their problems. He knows that the furthest star of the universe can shine in the nearest things, and this is why he shares his world with those he loves, his most cherished friends.

When he works with his alliance for a common goal, the Wise Salesman never forgets the contribution of a single members of the group, because the sweat of each one of them has become one with his along the way. He does not need anybody to remind him of the help he has received. He remembers on his own and rejoices with his companions for all the victories they reached together, sharing with them the reward. He can be grateful with those who deserve it. He can be grateful with those who supported and helped him, sharing his goal. The Wise Salesman never puts his interests before those of his friends.

The Wise Salesman always tries to inspire every member of his team. This is why he loves to talk to his friends about his successes. He tells enthusiastically about how he conquered his victories and how he overcame difficult moments. When he talks about his victories, he loves to use a passionate, romantic tone, indulging sometimes in small exaggerations. But he never commits the mistake of confusing pride with vanity. He does not really believe in his exaggerations. He just uses them to fire up the team.

The Wise Salesman never forgets the importance of celebration rituals. When his team achieves a success, he celebrates it with his companions. Even if it is just a temporary success, he knows that celebrating it can inspire great self-confidence. Victory cost sacrifices, hardships, nights of doubt, and days of waiting. It is good to celebrate it. The Wise Salesman celebrates today the victories of yesterday to have more confidence tomorrow.

The Wise Salesman is patient with all the members of his alliance. He knows that everyone has their own adaptation times; therefore, he is not surprised at their change of attitude. He waits for everybody to justify their actions and explain their behaviour. After all, the path to success is never plain, and it is necessary to expect the unexpected, to which everybody may react differently. Sometimes, the difficulties of the way cause fights and arguments inside the team. Sometimes, the allies accuse each other. But eventually everyone goes back to rowing in the same direction again, forgetting the offences. The Wise Salesman is ready to discuss but also works for harmony to return.

An alliance is almost never composed of a fixed number of people. Sometimes, the passing of time, the victories, and even the defeats bring new collaborators. Since they do not have a common history with the rest of the group, they initially tend to show only their qualities, so much so that many believe they are as sage as masters. But the Wise Salesman, as glad as he is to welcome them, never makes the mistake of comparing them with his old companions. He will fully trust the newcomers only after discovering their defects. He never works with somebody without knowing their limits first.

The Wise Salesman works hard to gather faithful allies around him, trying to understand their strengths and weaknesses. Nevertheless, sometimes it happens that one of his allies turns into an enemy. Initially, hate pervades him. But he immediately gets rid of this feeling, because hate blinds and never leads to any benefit, only to misfortune and destruction. Then he reconsiders the nice moments he shared with his ex-companion and examines whether his leadership was just, his actions correct, and his strategy effective. He tries to understand the reasons for such a breakup. The Wise Salesman never takes for granted that whatever he does is good. This is why he profits from every situation to become a better person.

The Wise Salesman also knows that no alliance lasts forever. Sometimes, in order to accomplish his goal, he must necessarily join a new group, abandoning the old one. Whenever an alliance comes to an end, the Wise Salesman thanks his companions, and feeling sorry about having to leave them, he carries on towards his destiny, keeping in his heart the wonderful memories of an unforgettable experience.

If you would win a man to your cause, first convince him that you are his sincere friend. Therein is a drop of honey that catches his heart, which, say what he will, is the great high-road to his reason, and which, when once gained, you will find but little trouble in convincing his judgment of the justice of your cause, if indeed that cause really be a just one.

—ABRAHAM LINCOLN

Chapter 10

THE FRUITFUL MANAGEMENT OF TIME

The Wise Salesman achieves the results he was hoping for because he plans his life, managing the time on hand in the best way possible. He knows that nobody can stop the inexorable hourglass of time, but everybody can accurately organize their days to make them marvelously fruitful and useful for the accomplishment of the goal. Time never stops, but it can be managed. The first thing to do is to divide it in a balanced way according to the three great needs: work, health, and leisure.

The Wise Salesman reckons that in order to preserve one's health, it is necessary to sleep about eight hours a day; to achieve one's professional goals one must work

· eight to ten hours a day; to enjoy leisure time, six to eight hours a day are enough. Distributing time, though, is not enough to achieve success. What really counts is the quality of the activities one occupies his hours with.

The Wise Salesman was not always free to do what he really loved. At times it happened that he hated the things he was forced to do. He could not avoid doing them because they were necessary in his daily life. In those moments, he surely wished for something different. An ardent desire was burning in his soul, but he was a prisoner. He felt like he was living two lives at the same time. In one life, he had to do all he did not want to do, to meet people who did not enrich him in the least, and to fight for ideas he did not believe in. But there was a second life. It was the one he discovered in his dreams, in the depths of his spirit, in the melancholic readings of a life he was not living, in the meetings with people who thought the same way he did and who could promote him both spiritually and materially. And this could happen only in his leisure time. But he discovered the secret to join these two lives, making them coincide more and more. He began to use his free time to get ready for something better, because that was the time for opportunities, since his working time absorbed him completely and killed his dreams. He started to cultivate positive friendships and fruitful relationships that could satisfy him in all sectors of his life. He began to frequent people who would recognize his value and help him accomplish his goal. He met friends who rescued him from the abyss of mediocrity, allowing him to soar up to the peaks of success. Sowing the seed of opportunities during his leisure time, the Wise Salesman waited for it to blossom and grow: what he did was build a bridge between what he was doing and what he would have liked to do. He made the most of all his free time, and slowly, the ardent desires got hold of his life, until he felt he was ready for what he had always dreamed of. At that point, he did not need much to finally join his two lives together, making them one.

The Wise Salesman is good at cultivating friendships so that they enrich him. He tends to never spend a single moment of his life with people who cannot help him in any way. This habit is positive and constructive. It absolutely does not stem from an egotistic will. It rather blossoms naturally and spontaneously in his social relationships, which are based not only on receiving but also on giving. The Wise Salesman never interacts with other people without giving them something in return. Often he benefits his neighbour with an equivalent or even greater service than what he received. For every material and spiritual treasure he gathers, he helps others gain as much. He helps his friends when they are in difficulty and never forgets to gift part of his goods to those who need them more than he does. He is a generous person, never self-centred, although he surrounds himself only with people he considers to be positive for his existential growth. He would indeed be egotistic, on the contrary, if he wasted his precious time, subtracting it from his loved ones and from his dearest collaborators, to follow negative, useless, or even destructive habits. He calls egotistic those who live for themselves without ever giving anything in return—those who despise without reason both their time and that of the others and those who spend their life enjoying the advantages of civilization without ever assuming any responsibility or contributing to the source of those advantages. Unlike them, the Wise Salesman uses his time in a considered and constructive way, never wasting it with idle people who lack ambition and let themselves fall into awful habits. He does not allow anything and anyone to steal his precious time. By choosing the right people to interact with, he not only preserves the quality of his days but also behaves altruistically, because he enriches himself and above all those he spends time with.

The Wise Salesman believes that whoever wastes his time is a sinner. He always bears in mind the words of Bernard Berenson: "Killing time, rather than using it as the true essence of an experienced and not just passed life, is certainly the sin of sins."

The Wise Salesman can turn his time into anything he wishes for. He does not simply fill his life with moments; he fills his moments with life, making his dreams come true. Once his goal is accomplished, whatever it may be, the passing of time will not count, because it will not be needed anymore. The only important thing will be the infinite depth of each moment. And this is why the Wise Salesman is destined for eternal happiness.

There is nothing more precious than time, because it is the price for eternity.

—LOUIS BOURDALOUE

EPILOGUE

*A*ll along his way to success, however far he drifted in the flow of life, the Wise Salesman never for a moment forgot the merchant he had met as a young man. It was thanks to him that he had discovered the secret to reach the greatest of all riches: happiness. When on that magical day he had asked what he had to do to become a great salesman, the merchant had replied: "If you are here, it is because you heard I am the greatest merchant in the world. Do you have any idea why?"

"I think it is because of all this extraordinary and unique merchandise around us," the boy answered.

The wise man went on: "I am the greatest merchant in the world because I learned to gather something people often forget about, on the market as well as in life. I learned to gather happiness. All you see here is nothing but an expression of the marvels of the world. All this

merchandise is nothing but a mirror of the thousand beauties of life. People seek happiness, and happiness does not come from one source only. At times, they can be happy about deep and important things. At times, the simplest thing is enough. You will find happiness in the emotions and feelings of other people, in the wonders of nature, and in the skilfully crafted creations of man. You will have to be very careful not to miss any of the wonders nature and the human genius have to offer you, however big or distant they may be. You will have to learn how to love and burst with joy for such a powerful emotion. You will have to learn to rejoice at the beauty of a sunset and to be enchanted by a painting. But at the same time, you will never have to forget about the details and the small things. You will have to stay focused on the daily life surrounding you without neglecting a single one of your days. When you become able to do both things without letting one overwhelm the other, then you will have gathered a special sensitivity, which will make you happy and will help you understand the importance of making others happy. Pay attention to this truth, because I cannot tell you exactly what to do. I do not know your deepest dreams. I'm ignorant of what success you yearn for. There are many definitions of success and everybody has their own peak to climb. And not all peaks of success are at the same height. But I can tell you a secret, and you can apply it to any goal you choose to strive for: You will
. be a Wise Salesman only if you become happy while

making others happy. The moment you stop filling your own cup of happiness and start excelling in life, filling up the cup of the other people too, you will find that your cup stays full, and you will be amazed. Now go, and start gathering your happiness!"

ABOUT THE AUTHOR

$\mathcal{F}$rank Pacino graduated with top grades in economics with an emphasis in management. He began working early, during his college years. At the age of 20, he started his own entrepreneurial activity. Later on he continued to work in several fields, always as self-employed, from sales to service to marketing and communication consulting. He has worked for several daily newspapers, writing a few economic columns, and for some publishing houses, with projects about culture, sociology, and production. In addition to his work activity, which has shaped him as an entrepreneur and communicator, he has taken an interest in motivational literature. In particular, he has concentrated on the philosophy of personal success, discovering a new universe that greatly helped him improve both at the spiritual and professional level. Thus, he started a new life. Having acquired a thorough knowledge of the achievement of personal success, both in theory and in practice, he wished to divulge it and put it at everybody's disposal, since he believes excellence is a universal right. Therefore, he decided to pursue a career in writing.

Frank Pacino is the author of the book *The Wise Salesman*.

CONTACT FRANK PACINO

Website:
www.frankpacino.com

Email:
info@frankpacino.com

Facebook:
facebook.com/FrankPacinoWins

Twitter:
@FrankPacinoWins

CPSIA information can be obtained at www.ICGtesting.com
Printed in the USA
LVOW06s0019050116

469132LV00001B/62/P